Traditions Around The World
Costumes

by Danielle Sensier

Wayland

Traditions Around The World

Other titles in the Traditions Around The World series:

Body Decoration

Dance

Food

Games

Jewellery and Accessories

Masks

Musical Instruments

Series editor: James Kerr

Designer: Loraine Hayes

Consultant: Anthony Shelton, Keeper of Non-Western Art and Anthropology, Royal Pavilion Art Gallery and Museums, Brighton.

First published in 1994 by Wayland (Publishers) Ltd
61 Western Road, Hove, East Sussex
BN3 1JD, England

© Copyright 1994 Wayland (Publishers) Ltd

British Library Cataloguing in Publication Data

Sensier, Danielle
  Costumes. - (Traditions Around the World Series)
  I. Title II. Series
  391.009

ISBN 0 7502 1222 5

Typeset by Loraine Hayes Design
Printed and bound in Italy by G. Canale and C.S.p.A.

COVER: Traditional garments of the Rajasthan region in North-West India.

Picture acknowledgements:

The publishers wish to thank the following for providing the photographs for this book: Bryan & Cherry Alexander 15; Bruce Coleman Limited 14-15, 16-17 (Erwin & Peggy Bauer), 18 (Charles Henneghien), 34-5 (Gerald Cubitt); Sue Cunningham Photographic 12, 20-21, 25; Robert Estall 28-9 (Angela Fisher & Carol Beckwith), 30-31 (Carol Beckwith); Eye Ubiquitous COVER (David Cumming); 10 (G.R. Richardson), 16 (L. Fordyce), 27 (Tony Brown), 35 (top) (David Cumming), 36 (top) (Paul Thompson), 36 (bottom) (P.M. Field), 38-9 (David Cumming), 44-5 (Matthew McKee); Jimmy Holmes 6, 6-7, 7; Life File 8-9 (Emma Lee), 24-5 (Juliet Highet), 37 (Paul Fisher), 39 (Hiroshi Isobe); Link 13 (Orde Eliason), 26-7 (Eric Meacher), 35 (bottom) (Shari Kessler), 41 and 42-3 (Orde Eliason); Photri 14, 16, 18 (top); South American Pictures 21, 22 and 22-3 (Tony Morrison); Still Pictures 30-31 (Mark Edwards); Tony Stone Worldwide 8 (Ken Welsh), 12-13 (David Hanson); Tropix 28 (D. Davis), 42 (D. Charlwood); Wayland Picture Library 11, 45.

The artwork is by Peter Bull.

Contents

Costumes around the world

NORTH AMERICA

SOUTH AMERICA

EUROPE

ASIA

AFRICA

THE PACIFIC

Introduction

Would you call your clothing traditional costume? You might be wearing modern clothes, but the style, material or pattern of them may be part of a costume that is hundreds of years old. It could even come from a country thousands of kilometres away.

Traditional clothing or costume is a type of dress that is worn by people who share the same nationality, religion or customs, and it may remain the same for many centuries.

We can look at traditional clothes and costumes and discover all sorts of interesting information about the history and beliefs of the people who wear them. A thousand ancient stories are woven into the fabric of the costumes of people around the world. As well as giving us clues about the wearer's beliefs and customs, traditional dress can also tell us something about the climate that people live in, the kinds of material they are able to use, and even the type of work they do.

These women from ▲ western China are dressed up for a wedding. Their head-dresses are traditional, but some of the women also wear modern coats, with western-style buttons and lapels.

◄ The clothes of these Rajasthani women in Pushkar, India, are embroidered with gold and silver thread. Instead of using a needle, the stitches are often made with a traditional tool called an *ari*.

Traditional costumes are often made in special ways, using methods that have been passed down from generation to generation. The ways in which clothes are sewn, woven and printed can be unique to a particular people. Designs and patterns of clothes often have special meanings. In Central Asia, a tulip motif is popular on some garments. In certain parts of this region, the tulip is the first flower to appear in the spring. It is a symbol of the happiness and new life that spring brings each year, so it is used decoratively to brighten clothing.

The colours of clothes can also tell us something about the people who wear them. In the Middle East, some clothes are decorated with blue beads or buttons. The wearer believes these will protect him or her against evil.

Certain costumes are worn by people for ceremonies such as weddings or funerals, and again the clothes can have special meanings. In many western countries, people wear black clothes to show that someone has died. Black or dark clothes are worn as a mark of respect for the dead person.

In some parts of the world, the clothes people wear every day are very traditional. They are the same style and use the same materials and designs as pieces of clothing worn many years ago. However, in many places special costumes are only worn on certain occasions. The clothes which people wear every day only hint at past traditions.

By using traditional designs, patterns and materials, we can add old meaning to modern clothes. By wearing traditional clothes or dressing up in costumes on special occasions, we are keeping some of the stories and customs of the past alive today.

▲ **Traditional clothes are made from all kinds of natural materials, including plant fibres. These hand-made sandals are made from plaited grass.**

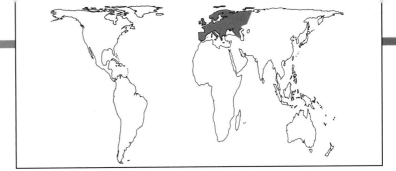

▲ These Polish street musicians are wearing folk costumes. The style and colour of the men's trousers and the flower designs on the woman's costume are traditional.

◀ Spanish flamenco dancers wear exciting costumes to match their lively dance routines. It is usual for the dresses to have fancy, colourful sleeves, and for women to wear real or silk flowers in their hair.

Europe

In Europe there are many different kinds of traditional clothes and costumes. A lot of them are connected with the country or area in which people live. Although few traditional costumes are now worn every day, people still wear them on special occasions or to do certain jobs.

Wearing a traditional costume gives people a sense of belonging to a certain group. Throughout history, a great many Europeans have left their original countries and cultures and have gone to live in other countries around the world. Wearing traditional costumes has helped these people and their ancestors to remember, and to let other people know, where they originally came from. In some cases, people's ways of life have changed a great deal. Wearing traditional costumes helps people to remember a way of life that they may not want to forget.

In some countries in Eastern Europe, such as Poland, people are keeping alive the traditions of folk music, dance and art that began in small farming communities many years ago. These people wear beautiful costumes to dance to folk music during festivals, or on special occasions such as weddings. At wedding ceremonies in the town of Krakow, the bridegroom wears a special head-dress covered with motifs of flowers and peacocks. These are symbols of good luck.

Traditional costumes are still worn for many kinds of dances. In Spain, flamenco dancers wear special costumes. Flamenco dancing is very graceful and exciting to watch. It can be seen at many festivals. The women wear brightly coloured dresses with lots of frills and flounces and the men wear tight-fitting trousers and bolero jackets. Spanish gypsies, called *gitanos*, are thought to be the best flamenco dancers. The style of costume worn by dancers originally came from the gypsies.

▲ This herdsman from Lapland in northern Scandinavia wears the traditional red and blue colours of the Saami costume. Thick layers of clothing and a fur hat keep him warm in the cold climate.

Nomadic peoples often have types of traditional dress that are very important to them. As they do not live in one place all of the time, feeling that they are part of a group with their own traditions is important. By wearing a traditional costume, they are keeping some of their past history alive.

The Saami people of Scandinavia were originally nomadic. They herded reindeer, moving from place to place to find good grazing ground for the animals. Today, some Saami still herd reindeer, and they wear traditional Saami clothing of warm woollen capes and special scarves and hats. Other Saami now live in different countries, often hundreds of kilometres away from each other. They still share the same customs and language. To keep their traditions alive, they cross countries to meet together for special reunions and on these occasions they wear elaborate costumes in traditional colours.

Sometimes the materials used to make clothes are part of a tradition. In Scotland, the kilt is a kind of skirt worn by men for Highland dancing and on special occasions. Scottish army regiments also wear kilts as part of their ceremonial uniforms. Each kilt has a chequered pattern on it called tartan. There are lots of different tartans, each one belonging to a different Scottish clan. The tartan tells people which clan a Scottish person's family belonged to originally.

While certain costumes can be the traditional dress of a country, some people wear traditional clothes to show that they see themselves as a group that is different from the other people in a country. In France there is an area called Brittany. Some of the people who live there do not want to be ruled by the French government. They would like to be independent. At local festivals such as the fishermen's fête at Concarneau, the Bretons wear traditional costume to show that they feel different to the people living in the rest of France. The women wear dresses with white cotton aprons and tall bonnets made from stiff white linen, decorated with embroidery or lace. The men wear boleros and breeches, and black, roll-brimmed hats.

◀ **A Scottish kilt**.

Using costume to express proud feelings about a place is also popular in European countries that were once ruled by a different country but are now independent. Latvia is a country that used to be part of the former USSR. Now it is independent and the Latvians are bringing back some of their old traditions. There is an old Latvian proverb that says 'what is red is beautiful' so traditional costumes are often decorated with red embroidery. The national costume for Latvian women includes a wide-sleeved blouse and full skirt, with a long, fringed headscarf and special sandals called *pastali*.

People with special jobs or who belong to a particular group can sometimes be identified by their traditional costumes. In Greece, the guardsmen outside the parliament building are easily recognizable because of their unusual skirts, stockings and shoes.

In Mediterranean ▶ countries, such as Italy and Portugal, many older women continue to wear black clothes long after the funeral of a relative - and sometimes for the rest of their lives.

Main picture: The uniform of these Greek guardsmen is a sign of their special status, which sets them apart from other people. The skirts are part of an ancient Greek costume, no longer worn by ordinary people in Greece today.

▲ This man lives in Britain, although his family comes from India. The turban wrapped around his head shows that he follows the Indian Sikh religion.

In many European countries people are studying traditional costumes in order to understand more about how people lived in the past. Although modern clothing in Europe looks very similar in each country, many of the styles and fabrics have traditional origins. Capital cities in Europe such as Paris, Rome and London are famous fashion centres of the world, where designers create new clothes and new 'looks'. Yet the clothes are not always as modern as they look because the ideas that designers use are often taken from traditional costumes.

Today there are many groups of people who have gone to live in Europe from other parts of the world. The costumes that they take with them help them to remember their customs and help to make the clothes and costumes that can be seen in Europe more rich and varied.

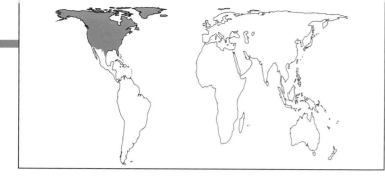

North America

The USA and Canada are homes to people from many different countries and cultures, so there are hundreds of different types of traditional dress. A lot of these clothes come from people who left Europe and took their traditions with them to North America. The other main types of traditional clothing come from Native American peoples, who have lived in these lands for thousands of years.

Long before the European settlers arrived in the sixteenth century, Native Americans in the Great Plains hunted buffalo for clothing and food. The skins of the buffalo were scraped clean and then tanned and dried, and the hooves were boiled down and used to make varnish for the hides. These were made into large robes, with colourful scenes from daily life or stories of great warriors painted on to them with natural dyes.

Some of the ancestors of these original peoples have kept old traditions going and they make handicrafts and clothes using ancient methods. Keeping these ways alive is important because some of the traditions are connected with the Native Americans' religious beliefs and stories which are thousands of years old.

▲ A traditional Navajo blanket is woven on a loom made from tree trunks. Many textiles and crafts made in traditional ways are now sold to tourists, providing an important source of income.

◀ This costume, worn by a chief of the Stoney people of Canada, includes a special harness for his horse. Notice the traditional use of feathers, beaded fringes and bold, geometric patterns.

The Navajo people who came from the south-west of the USA are very skilled weavers. They believe that a traditionally woven blanket becomes like a part of nature. Navajo blankets were originally woven on looms made out of tree trunks. These were held in place by rocks, and as they were woven, the blankets appeared to grow out of the earth. This is similar to the story of their ancestors. The Navajo believe that their people once lived beneath the earth and grew out of the ground. According to the story, the first person to teach the Navajo to weave was one of these ancestors, called Spider Woman.

These brightly coloured 'eye-dazzler' blankets are still part of Navajo traditional costume. Originally, the wool used to make the blankets was dyed using a mixture of berries, roots and minerals. Red dye was difficult to produce, but a solution came when the European settlers arrived. Blankets belonging to Europeans contained red wool, and the Navajo unravelled this and used it for their own new costumes.

The encounter between the first European settlers and Native Americans also influenced the clothing of the settlers. Native Americans in the north-west of the USA and Canada wore leggings and moccasins made from the furs and skins of deer, beavers and foxes. The settlers started to wear some of these warm clothes too, such as beaver-skin hats.

**Just like his husky dog, this Inuit man ▶
from Canada is kept warm by a fur coat.**

In the far north of Canada and in parts of Alaska, near to the Arctic, the Inuit peoples have traditional clothing that reflects the cold conditions in which they live. Today they wear waterproof clothing, made from modern materials, that is made thousands of kilometres away, but on long hunting expeditions some Inuit wear traditional clothes because they are considered to be warmer.

Traditional Inuit clothes are made from the skins and furs of animals found in the area where they live, such as seals, polar bears, caribou and Arctic foxes. The clothing has a double layer of animal skin. The inner layer is worn with the fur facing in and the outer layer with the fur facing out. The Inuit were the inventors of a coat called the *parka*, which has been adapted into a style of warm jacket in other parts of the world. The traditional parka is made from seal skin, and has a fur-lined hood, which makes it warm, waterproof and lightweight.

The everyday work clothing of early European settlers in North America created many new types of clothes which are now considered to be traditional. The workwear of cowboys in the West was hardwearing and practical. They wore cotton or wool shirts, strong leather boots and blue denim jeans reinforced with copper rivets. Denim jeans are now worn all over the world. Hats like those worn by the original cowboys are still worn by people today in some of the southern states of the USA, especially Texas. They are called stetsons, after a hat maker from Philadelphia called John B. Stetson. He began to produce this type of hat in the 1870s.

A Canadian Mountie. ▶

◀ **Modern-day cowboys wearing denim jeans and stetson hats at a rodeo competition in South Dakota, USA.**

Some traditional outfits have been used to create a strong national symbol. In Canada, the traditional uniform of the Canadian Mounted Police, who are known as Mounties, is very famous. The original Mounties were famously brave law enforcers in the backwoods of Canada. They wore bright-red uniforms and distinctive helmets. In the nineteenth century, pictures of Mounties were used to try to attract new settlers to Canada. Although the role of the Mounties is very different today, they are a symbol of national pride for Canadians.

Many North Americans whose ancestors came from Europe have traditional European national or local costumes that they wear for special festivals. The Amish people of Pennsylvania are descended from a group of Protestant Christians who migrated from Germany and Switzerland in the late 1600s. They wear very traditional clothes because of their religious customs. They reject modern manufactured things such as cars and telephones, and they believe that it is important to be humble in front of God. Bright, colourful clothes with fancy buttons and decorations are thought to be offensive to God. Both the men and women wear plain, dark-coloured clothes and hats, fastened with simple hooks or strings.

◀ **Amish children in traditional simple, plain clothing.**

The Amish were originally persecuted in some parts of Europe for their beliefs. They settled in America to get away from people who would not accept them. By continuing to wear their traditional clothing, they are telling people that they wish to keep their views and traditions, no matter how much the world around them changes.

In New York and other cities in North America, there is another religious group who also went to America to escape persecution. This is a group of Hasidic Jews, whose ancestors migrated from Europe. Hasidic Jews in New York live together in one district and have many

This young boy can be ▶ recognised straight away as a Hasidic Jew. In keeping with his religious beliefs, the sides of his hair have not been cut and his head is covered by a cap.

ancient religious beliefs and customs. The men wear distinctive black coats and hats and do not cut the sides of their hair. When they are not wearing their hats they keep their heads covered with a small cap called a *kippah* or *yarmulke*. During some religious services, they wear small black boxes called *tefillin* on the forehead or left arm. These contain writings from the Jewish holy book, called the *Torah*.

It is also important in their culture that women are not vain, so they always dress modestly and keep their heads covered. When they marry, women wear wigs in public. These traditional Jews have also settled in other places such as Jerusalem in Israel. They wear exactly the same costumes there as in New York. Like the Amish in Pennsylvania, they are following traditions for which they were once persecuted.

It is sometimes difficult to understand the beliefs of these religious groups. By learning about their customs, such as their traditional costumes, we can find out why their traditions are so important to them.

Project: Making a Native American Head-band

You will need:
tapestry cloth (or sacking)
old leftover wool (3 different colours)
large-eyed tapestry needle
scissors

1. Cut the cloth to a width of 65 cm. This may vary depending on the size of the cloth holes. The suggested design needs 27 holes from top to bottom, plus a small space at either edge. Cut the cloth long enough to fit around your forehead, leaving a small space at the back of your head.

2. Work the embroidery using lengths of the wool. Follow the suggested design by counting the coloured squares - 1 square = 3 holes in the canvas.

3. Thread the needle. To make a stitch, pass the needle through one hole working from back to front.

   Make a long straight stitch covering three holes, and pass the needle back through the canvas from front to back.

At the back of the canvas, pass the needle in a slanting position and then through the hole next to the bottom of the previous stitch.

Your needle is now at the front of the canvas again, and you are ready to make the next stitch.

4. Repeat the suggested design until you have covered the length of the canvas, and fasten any loose ends. Thread and knot a length of wool at each end of the canvas and tie in a bow to secure the band around your forehead.

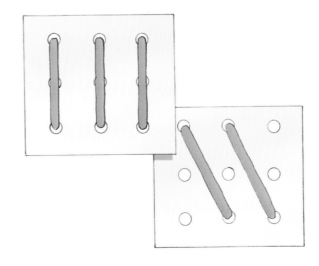

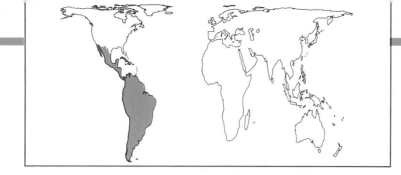

Central and South America

From clothes which are decorated using crushed beetles to bowler hats, South and Central America, like North America, has a fascinating mix of traditional clothes and costumes. Some come from European settlers, while others have their origins in the dress of the original Amerindian peoples, and still more are a mixture of these two cultures.

The ancient civilizations of South America – the Mayans, Aztecs and Incas – valued textiles very highly. The Aztecs and Mayans even worshipped a goddess of weaving. The Aztecs would demand fine clothes and dyes from the peoples they conquered. The Incas demanded taxes from people in the form of woven cloth, costumes and dyes. These were given to the army and important people.

In modern Guatemala, around half of the population are descendants of the ancient Mayans. In some areas people still weave textiles on traditional back-strap looms, just like their ancestors. Some women wear clothes today which are similar to those shown on ancient Mayan carvings.

The main part of the traditional Guatemalan costume for women is a straight, loose blouse called a *huipil*, worn with a wrap-around skirt. Each village has its own huipil design, with distinctive colours and patterns.

Hats of many different styles are popular all over South and Central America. These felt hats are from Ecuador, and are made from llama wool. ▼

Many of the traditional ▶ clothes of Central and South America are made from wool which has been spun by hand. In the highlands of Peru, women use a simple drop-spindle - rather like a spinning top - instead of a spinning wheel. It is easy to carry and can be used anywhere.

The women wear a *tzute* on their heads. This is a woven length of material that is worn as a loose flat turban, or used for carrying loads.

In the San Blas Islands of Panama, some Kuna women still wear their traditional Amerindian costume every day. The Kuna women developed a style of appliqué which is used to make the *mola.* This is a blouse made from sewing layers of brightly coloured embroidered cloth on to other bits of cloth. Each woman has several mola blouses, which she starts to make when she is a girl at school. New designs to be worn for a special occasion are usually made in secret, and are hidden beneath an old mola until the last moment. Traditional mola motifs include plants, animals, dreams and scenes from everyday life,

These Kuna women are dressed up for a ▲ special occasion, so they are wearing their best clothes. Look at the brightly coloured cloth and hundreds of intricate stitches on their *mola* blouses.

but today's designs include modern images such as spaceships and Coca-Cola bottles.

High up in the Andean mountains of Peru and Bolivia live the Aymara people. In country areas, they still wear traditional clothes. The women wear *polleras*. These are several skirts made from brightly coloured cotton, worn one on top of another. If a woman wears a number of full skirts it is a sign of wealth. The women also wear a brightly striped cotton shawl called an *aguayo*, which is handy for carrying babies.

In the Andean mountains, people use hats to keep them warm at night and to shade them from the hot sun during the day. The Aymara men wear brightly coloured knitted hats with flaps to keep their ears covered. In Bolivia, *chola* women, who are part-Spanish and part-Amerindian, wear bowler hats. These hats came from Britain, where they were very popular in the middle of the nineteenth century. Many of the British men who came to Bolivia to work on the railways wore bowler hats and the women adopted the style. They are now traditional wear.

◀ **These Aymara Indians in Bolivia are wearing traditional hats, shawls and skirts. Their *pollera* skirts are also popular for dancing as they are designed to swirl when spun.**

Wool from local animals such as llamas or alpaca has always been used in traditional Amerindian dress. When the Spanish arrived in South America, they brought merino sheep with them. The merino sheep produces a fine, silky wool. It became popular with Amerindians as it is easy to spin. In Mexico, some of the most beautiful *serapes* - which are rectangular pieces of fabric used as cloaks and blankets - and *ponchos* are made from tightly spun merino wool. Today most of these traditional clothes are coloured using modern dyes. But Mexico is famous for one of its traditional dyes. It is a crimson dye called cochineal, because it is made by crushing the small cochineal beetle. The insects have to be farmed on a large scale. As it is so difficult to make, the dye is very valuable to people who want to use natural colours.

In South America and the Caribbean, there are other groups of people who use dress to say something about their identity. From the sixteenth to the nineteenth century, European settlers brought in Africans to work for them as slaves. Some of their descendants remember the history of slavery at huge events called carnivals. Carnival celebrations first began in Christian Europe. They were held in order to have fun, break rules and feast just before the period of Lent. Carnival became popular in the Caribbean in the eighteenth century. Just for the day, slaves were allowed to be masters, men dressed as women, and there was music and dancing, which were normally forbidden.

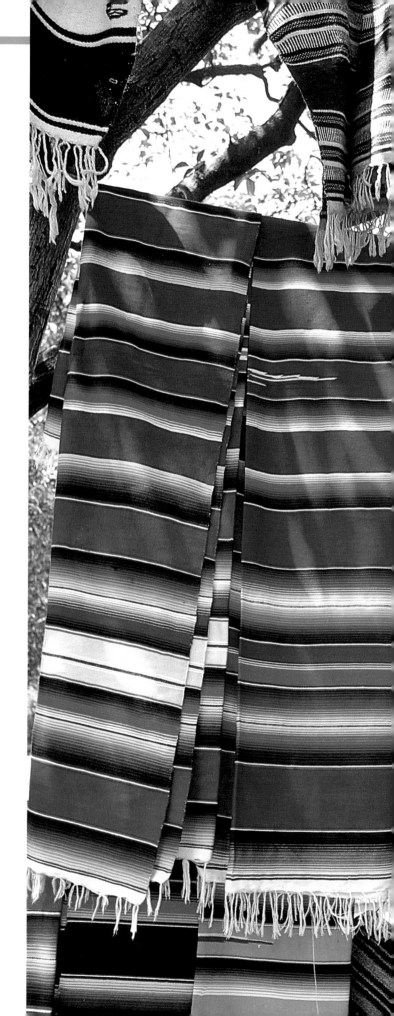

24

Traditionally, carnival costumes are used to show the struggles of people for freedom. On the Caribbean island of Trinidad, and in some parts of South America, this traditional meaning can still be seen. Many of the costumes are designed to remind people of the cruel treatment of the African slaves in the past. Other costumes are used to criticize politicians today.

Carnivals are also held in parts of America such as New Orleans in the USA and Rio de Janeiro in Brazil. The costumes at these carnivals rarely show the struggle of slaves for freedom. The themes of the costumes change all the time, and the designs are so fabulous that people come from around the world to watch the processions. The tradition of dressing up in costume and celebrating, which began about 200 years ago, is being continued.

◄ **This carnival costume from Rio de Janeiro symbolises the terrible cruelty of slavery. It was not unusual for African slaves to be tied up with chains and collars.**

◄ **Mexican blankets, called serapes, feature distinctive bold, colourful stripes. Many are exported to other parts of the world, or sold to tourists.**

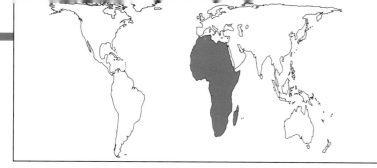

Africa

Africa is home to many different cultures and countries. It spans thousands of kilometres and the climate and natural materials available vary greatly in different parts of the continent. Religious beliefs, politics and trade with foreign countries have all affected traditional clothing.

Traditional African textiles are made from a wide variety of natural materials. As well as cotton and animal skins, there are some special plant fibres that can be made into cloth. Raffia is a kind of palm tree that has a useful fibre in the stalk of its leaves. This is used for weaving in traditional cloth. Another plant fibre that was used in parts of Uganda is tree bark. The bark was wrapped in banana leaves and steamed over a small fire. This made the bark change from brown to a rich golden colour. The bark was then beaten to soften it.

In the countries of West Africa, people have been producing and trading in woven textiles for hundreds of years. As far back as the sixteenth century, cotton cloth from northern Nigeria was brought by camel across the huge Sahara desert to the coast, where it was shipped to countries all around the Mediterranean Sea. This trade still continues today.

▲ The Nilotic people from Kenya wear simple wrap-around garments. Women decorate the beaded collars and head-dresses.

In West Africa, thin strips of cloth are woven by men using ▶ traditional looms. They are then sewn together to make large pieces of material, used for a variety of garments.

The Yoruba people of Nigeria make a traditional patterned cloth called *adire*, for long, wrap-around garments and turbans. The tie-dye pattern is made by tying or stitching the cloth tightly with lengths of raffia before it is dyed. The stitched or tied areas of cloth are not touched by the dye, leaving a pale blue pattern on a dark blue background. The names given to the different types of patterns include local proverbs, such as 'the lazy man cannot be proud'.

Throughout Africa, both men and women are involved in making traditional clothing, but they tend to do different jobs. In Morocco, spinning and weaving are thought to be women's work, while sewing up, embroidery and making tassels, braids and fringes are all done by men. Embroidery on leather is nearly always done by men. They also crochet and knit warm leggings and hats for themselves.

▲ These Tuareg men wear traditional clothing, which hides them from strangers and protects them from the desert dust.

The Hausa people of Nigeria wear large robes and baggy trousers. These garments are made and embroidered by men. Each stage of manufacture is carried out by a different specialist. Most designs are made up of two or more long triangular shapes called 'knives'. Traditional patterns are known by names such as the 'two knives' or the 'five knives' design.

In Ghana, *kente* cloth is only produced by men, who pass on the skill to their sons and brothers when they are three or four years old. It is believed that if women took part in the weaving or sewing processes, they would be unable to have children. The cloth is made from very thin strips of fabric woven on a narrow loom and stitched together. It can then be made up into clothing. The cloth is dyed and block-printed, and the most complicated designs are saved for religious occasions.

The beliefs of a group of people are often tied up in certain traditional costumes. In some places in Africa, special clothing is worn to protect the wearer against sickness, evil spirits or warriors in battle. Asante warriors once wore elaborate costumes decorated with special charms to protect them in battle.

◄ **This Beja woman from Eritrea is almost completely covered from head to toe.**

In East Africa, the Masai people of Kenya value their cattle very highly. The cattle are an important source of food, fuel and clothing, and no part of the animal is wasted. Masai women traditionally wear skirts made from strips of tanned and dried cow hide, decorated with small, brightly coloured beads. The wearing of traditional cow-hide skirts reflects the importance of the animal to the Masai.

The colours of costumes often have important meanings. Around the world, the meaning of certain colours can be very different. For the Chinese, red is a lucky colour. However, on the island of Madagascar off the east coast of Africa, red is the colour used for special burial clothes. In Ghana, red is worn for mourning. In Benin, red is worn as a symbol of warfare and power, and further east in Nigeria, it is a symbol of success.

Climate can determine the kind of clothes a group of people wear traditionally. The Sahara desert has a direct effect on the way the Tuareg people dress. Some are still nomads – constantly moving with their goats and camels to find new grazing land. To keep cool in the desert heat, they wear long, loose clothes which allow the air to move about. The men wear turbans which they can wrap round their faces and mouths to protect them against the desert sands and wind. Men who keep to the old Tuareg traditions wear veils when they are with women, strangers or their wife's relatives.

The preference for wearing long, loose clothes is also found amongst other nomadic peoples living in desert areas, such as the Bedouin and other groups living in countries in the Middle East.

Some African costumes reveal the influence European colonists once had in certain countries. In Madagascar, the costumes of traditional male dancers are in the style of the former French colonists. They wear narrow-brimmed hats, tight trousers, long jackets and bright cummerbunds round their waists. As people of African descent have come to live in other parts of the world, they have brought many of the bright, bold designs and styles of their traditional clothes with them. In turn, European and American-style clothing and designs are now common in many parts of Africa.

◀ **Coloured beads and cow hide are used to make the traditional clothes of the Masai people of Kenya.**

Main picture: The clothes of this Hausa girl from Nigeria are decorated with beautiful motifs.

Project: Making a Tie-dye Tee-shirt

You will need:
old white tee-shirt
wooden spoon
rubber gloves
tin of cold water dye
old plastic bowl
drying line
old newspaper
ball of string
old apron
measuring jug

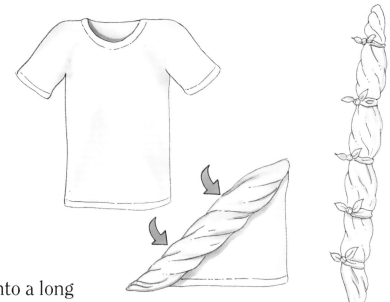

1. Fold and roll the tee-shirt into a long tight tube. Wind lengths of string around it at regular intervals and tie them into knots.

2. Put on the apron and gloves. Measure the correct amounts of water and dye, as instructed on the tin, and pour them into the bowl. Mix the solution well with the spoon.

3. Place the tee-shirt in the bowl of dye, making sure it is completely covered. Leave it to soak for the time given on the tin.

4. Hang the tee-shirt out to dry. If you are using an inside line, make sure you put down newspaper to catch the drips.

5. When it is completely dry, remove the string and see what patterns you have made.

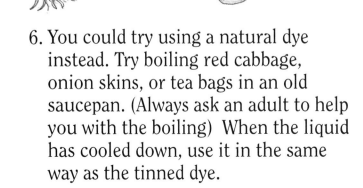

6. You could try using a natural dye instead. Try boiling red cabbage, onion skins, or tea bags in an old saucepan. (Always ask an adult to help you with the boiling) When the liquid has cooled down, use it in the same way as the tinned dye.

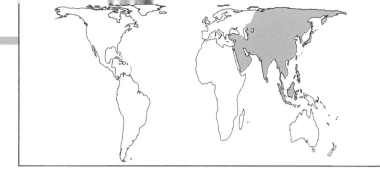

Asia

Asia is a treasure trove of beautiful traditional clothing, some of which dates back to ancient times. Silk from China has been produced and made into magnificent clothes for thousands of years. The art of traditional embroidery is so old in India that embroidery needles have been found that are 4,000 years old.

In some Asian countries, traditional costumes are very popular. A lot of importance is given to the ancient arts of needlework and other handicrafts. Girls may start to learn to sew from the age of six in the country areas of Pakistan, India and Bangladesh. One of the most elaborately decorated items a girl will work on is her wedding dress. Embroidery workshops exist in India, where men produce and sell embroidery. One of the most popular motifs of Indian embroidery is the elephant, which is a symbol of good luck.

Some of the traditional costumes in India, Pakistan and Afghanistan include a kind of mirror-work called *shishadur*. Poor people used to decorate their clothes with shiny beetle wings, which glimmered like the jewels of the rich. Eventually, these were replaced with tiny mirrors, which are still used today. The mirrors are used to decorate all kinds of costumes, from boys' caps to brides' shawls. Even animals are draped in *shisha* costumes for certain traditional events. Some people believe that wearing these clothes will frighten away evil spirits who will be scared by seeing their own reflection in the mirrors. Flowers, parrots and peacocks are favourite motifs for this type of traditional embroidery.

◀ In the region of Rajasthan, clothes worn on special occasions are richly embroidered with gold and silver thread. This woman's costume has also been decorated with silver discs which look like coins.

In northern Thailand and Burma each village has its own traditional clothes, which are sewn or embroidered. Tourists often buy this clothing. In other parts of Thailand some of the most beautiful traditional clothes are worn by dance groups. They are made from expensive silks in bright red, green and gold and are decorated with gold embroidery and beads. These costumes imitate the clothes worn at the royal court in Thailand in ancient times.

Main picture: An amazing variety of fabrics, motifs and handcrafts are used to make a traditional Indian *sari*. Can you tell which patterns have been made by embroidery and which have been made by block printing?

◀ Young girls from the hills of northern Thailand wear velvet costumes decorated with silver ornaments, tassels and pom-poms. At New Year, wearing new clothes is thought to bring good luck.

Another way of decorating clothing is found further south, in Indonesia. The *sarong* is a cool, traditional wrap-around skirt that is worn by men and women in this region. Sarongs are made from fabric decorated with *batik*, which is an Indonesian word that means 'wax writing'. Hot wax is applied to the material and when the fabric is dyed, only the areas without wax become coloured. The wax pattern is applied by hand with a special kind of pen or a metal stamp.

A traditional way of making patterns on Indian clothing is block printing. This is done by dipping a carved block of wood into a colour and stamping it on to the material. A pattern is made by repeating this action many times. Traditional *saris* are decorated in this way. The cotton sari is a length of cloth wound around the body and draped over one shoulder. It is worn by women all over India.

▲ This elaborate costume is worn by a temple dancer at a holy shrine in Bangkok, Thailand.

The *dhoti* is a cotton garment traditionally worn by men in India. It is a wide length of cotton that is wrapped around the waist, with the end pulled up and tucked between the legs.

Cotton is used to make many of the clothes worn by people in India. It grows well in the hot, moist climate. Cotton is easy to wear because it is cool and washable. Traditionally in India, cotton was spun by hand, but during the time in which India was ruled by Britain, manufactured cotton was imported from other countries. The great Indian leader Mahatma Gandhi used to wear a simple dhoti to show that he preferred

▲ These regimental turbans are worn by Indian soldiers in Calcutta. Like the man in the photograph on page 13, the soldiers are Sikhs.

traditional Indian hand-spun cotton garments to clothing which had been made from imported fabric. So the wearing of traditionally spun cotton clothing became an important symbol of Indian independence. Politicians continue to encourage people to hand-spin cotton today.

In the Middle East, clothing can also be used to show a point of view. Many Palestinians are forced to live in refugee camps far away from their traditional homelands. For some of these people, wearing traditional clothing is a way of keeping their way of life alive. Palestinian women traditionally wear an ankle-length robe or coat-dress, with a wide sash and a veil. The garment is decorated with cross-stitch embroidery, and at one time the colour and pattern of the embroidery showed which village the wearer came from.

Many Palestinians living in other countries prefer to wear western styles of dress, but they often still wear a *keffiyeh*, sometimes as a scarf. The keffiyeh is a red or black and white chequered traditional Arab head-dress. It is also worn by people as a symbol of their Palestinian identity.

Clothing can have both a political and religious meaning. Traditional Muslim women believe that the Islamic holy book, the Qur'an, tells them to be modest, so they wear clothes that cover their bodies almost completely. Wearing a *chador* or long black gown to hide almost all or part of their bodies is common among women who live in certain strict Muslim countries. Today, there are Muslim women around the world who used to wear western styles of clothing, but who now wear chadors. By doing this they are showing that they prefer Islamic values to western ideas and customs.

In north Yemen, a Muslim ▶ woman does not always cover her whole body in public. But in keeping with Muslim beliefs, her face is mostly covered by scarves as a sign of modesty.

In all parts of the world, religious groups have traditional costumes that may date back over many centuries. In Thailand, almost all young men at some time go to live in a Buddhist monastery. During this time, they stop wearing their ordinary clothing and wear a simple orange robe with no decorations. Dressing in this way helps the Buddhists to concentrate on their spiritual life instead of thinking about material things like clothes and fashion. Throughout Asia, the traditional orange robes of Buddhist monks let people know that the wearer is concentrating on his spiritual life.

In contrast to the humble robes of Buddhist monks are clothes made from Asia's most luxurious traditional material - silk. Real silk is made from the cocoon of a certain kind of caterpillar that lives in juniper trees. Silk is very warm, soft and strong. Mongolian soldiers in ancient times used to wear it next to their skin because it is so strong that an arrowhead could not pierce it. If a soldier got shot by an arrow, the silk cloth was driven into the wound, wrapped around the arrowhead. When the arrow was pulled out of the wound, the silk would have partly protected the soldier's body so that the wound was not too serious.

The Chinese were the first to discover this wonderful, soft thread and they guarded their secret so jealously that to take silk out of China was punishable by death. Eventually, ancient Chinese emperors became very rich by selling silk to the rest of the world.

For hundreds of years, silk was a symbol of wealth in China, but during this century there was a revolution against such luxuriousness. People began to see traditional silk clothing as part of an unfair system in China, where there were some people who were very rich and others who were very poor. Traditional Chinese clothes were decorated in a way that would tell people how important a person was. A dragon

◄ These young men are learning to be Buddhist monks, and are not allowed to own wealth of any kind. Their simple orange robes are given to them by their religious followers.

This Japanese *kimono* is ► made from expensive silk, tied with a complicated sash. Silk is one of the world's most comfortable fabrics - but perhaps a kimono is not ideal for playing in!

decoration with five claws showed that a person was more important than someone who was only allowed to wear a dragon decoration with four claws. After 1949, there were great political changes in China, and the Chinese way of life was changed in an attempt to make people more equal. People wore a simple uniform of plain working clothes. This was supposed to show that everyone was of equal importance.

Silk is also important in Japan. A silk *kimono* is a traditional part of a Japanese woman's national costume. The kimono is a loose robe wrapped over in the front and tied with a sash called an *obi*. The cocoons of 3,000 silk worms might be used to make one kimono. Kimonos are not usually worn every day, except by some older women. For weddings, women who choose to wear traditional dress will have a special kimono. They are often decorated with cranes, because this bird is an important symbol of happiness to Japanese people.

Although the Chinese lost their power as the only producers of silk, it is still mainly made in Asia. Now people from all around the world can enjoy wearing this traditional material.

Project: Making a Paisley Bandana

You will need:
large plain white handkerchief
fabric crayons
tracing paper
pencil
scissors
iron

These buta motifs were first printed on seventeenth-century Kashmir shawls, exported by the East India Company. They became so popular that soon European factories were copying them. The pattern became known as 'paisley' after the Scottish town of Paisley, which produced thousands of copies throughout the nineteenth century.

1. Cut a piece of tracing paper slightly larger than the handkerchief. Trace one or more of the suggested motifs on to it until you have covered the same area as the handkerchief. You can use any combination of motifs to make your own paisley design.

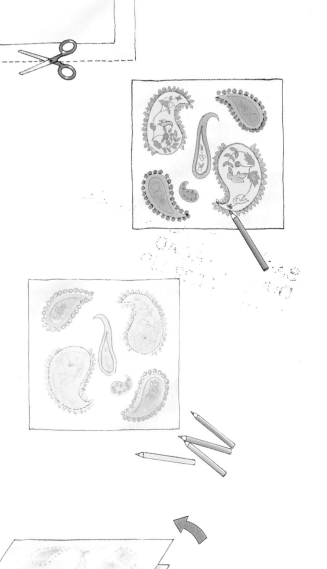

2. With the fabric crayons, outline and colour in your design on the tracing paper.

3. Iron the handkerchief flat. Reverse the tracing paper so that the design is face downwards, and place it over the top of the handkerchief.

4. Iron over the tracing paper to transfer the design on to the handkerchief. (Always ask an adult to help you with the ironing)

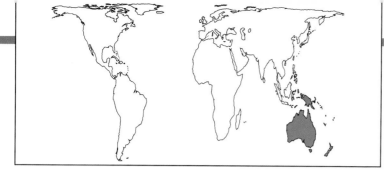

The Pacific

The Pacific is the region that includes Australia, New Zealand and thousands of different islands in the South Pacific Ocean. People lived on some of the islands for thousands of years without contact with the outside world. As a result, they developed their own languages, customs and traditional clothes without the influences of other cultures. For example, there are more than 700 different languages spoken on the islands of Papua New Guinea, and many different styles of traditional costume have developed.

As in other parts of the world, people use the natural materials in their area to make traditional clothing. On the islands of the Pacific, these include seeds, leaves, grasses, tree bark, shells, fur, feathers and sea creatures.

In the highlands of Papua ▶ New Guinea, bush people wear very little clothing. But elaborate head-dresses and collars are worn at traditional ceremonies. How many natural materials can you identify in this man's costume?

42

◀ The feathers and plumes of birds are an important part of many Pacific costumes.

Main picture: Barkcloth, called tapa, has been used to make this rain cape. The skirt is made from dried grasses.

As in Uganda, bark is used to make traditional costumes. In Papua New Guinea and the Pacific Islands, they take the inner bark of a mulberry tree and beat, dry and decorate it. This bark is called *tapa* and it is used to make a wrap-around garment worn by women, and also a kind of apron worn by men called a *malu*. For this, the bark is made into a narrow strip of fabric that hangs down from the waist. Malu are also made from dried grasses or woven material.

Among some of the highland peoples of Papua New Guinea there are important ceremonial pig hunts, which are followed by huge feasts. These festivals are a way of keeping traditional beliefs alive. Each group exchanges pigs and shells, and elaborate costumes are worn to show off the wearer's wealth and importance. Part of these costumes, especially for male dancers, includes leg and arm decorations made of clay, wood, shells and fur.

For fancy head-dresses, the feathers of birds are a favourite costume decoration in this part of the world. The Mekeo men, who live on the Papuan coast, wear huge head-dresses made from the colourful feathers of a beautiful creature called a bird of paradise. The head-dress of each village group has its own design, involving a complicated mixture of wood and feathers. In the Trobriand islands, traditional male dancers wear costumes made from the feathers of white cockatoos and black cassowary birds.

Today, some of these traditional costumes are made using modern sewing machines, instead of being made by hand. The materials included in the clothes of the Pacific region sometimes reflect more outside influences. An example of this is of a traditional grass skirt decorated with the labels from old tins. Grass skirts are a well-known type of traditional dress. On the Solomon islands and in Samoa, they are made from strips of banana leaves and dried in the sun. Then they are bound together on a waist band. Some parts of the skirt are dyed to produce multi-coloured stripes.

Another kind of traditional grass skirt is found on the Pacific island of Hawaii. This is part of the costume of the traditional *hula* dancers. Performers wear skirts made from green *ti* leaves, decorated bodices and flower garlands called *leis*. A more modern tradition, both for men who live in Hawaii and often for visitors, is to wear an *aloha* shirt. These are brightly coloured, short-sleeved shirts decorated with motifs such as parrots and palm trees. The shirts are so famous that they are known around the world as 'Hawaiian shirts'.

Both Australia and New Zealand were inhabited for thousands of years before European settlers started to move there two hundred years ago. In New Zealand the original Maori people, like the Australian Aborigines, normally wear modern clothing. However they are keen to keep their old traditions alive and wear special costumes to perform Maori dances. The costumes are made

from a woven flax called *taniko*. This is dyed black, yellow or a reddish-brown and is used to make a traditional skirt called a *piupi* that is worn by both men and women. In Australia, the Aboriginal peoples have few traditional costumes but instead decorate their bodies with paint for special occasions.

People from many different countries settled in Australia, and the ancestors of those settlers still feel a link with their various countries. Some of

◄ These Maori men are wearing traditional costumes to perform a ceremonial war dance called a *haka*. Such dances are part of the Maori's ancient customs, known as *Maoritanga*.

▲ These traditional Maori skirts, or *piupi*, would once have been worn on their own. But today's young Maori girls wear western-style shorts underneath.

them have national costumes, which they wear on traditional days. There is an area in the Barossa Valley in South Australia that was settled by a group of German immigrants. One of Australia's most popular wine festivals is held in this region, during which folk dancers wearing traditional leather breeches called *lederhosen* can be seen celebrating German traditions. In the city of Sydney, Greek women dancers wear colourful boleros, aprons and scarves to perform Greek dances during the special festivals. As in other parts of the world, there is not one, but many different costumes that belong in Australia today.

Although most of us wear modern clothes, traditional costumes have a special place in our world. They keep alive the memory of the world in which our different ancestors lived. Wearing traditional costume brings the past and present together in a beautiful way.

45

Glossary

Ancestors Dead relatives - often those living in ancient times.

Appliqué A type of embroidery using one or more layers of material.

Boleros Very short, tight-fitting jackets.

Breeches Half-length trousers gathered in at the knee.

Cassowary A New Guinea bird related to the emu.

Clan A family group.

Cummerbunds Wide sashes worn around the waist.

Fibres Fine strands from a plant or animal, which can be made into a textile.

Flounces Frilly strips of material sewn to a dress.

Folk Originating from, or traditional to, the people of one country or area.

Geometric Groups of simple shapes, points and lines.

Hide Animal skin.

Lent The forty days before Easter, when Christians fast in memory of Jesus Christ.

Looms Machines used to weave cloth.

Manufacture To make something, often in a factory.

Mass-produce To make a large number of goods using machines.

Merino A breed of sheep.

Middle East The area around the East Mediterranean, especially Israel and the Arab countries.

Migrate To move with your family to live in a different part of the world.

Moccasins Soft leather shoes without a heel, originally worn by Native American people.

Motif A repeated shape or picture used as decoration.

National costume The traditional clothes of one country.

Nomadic Moving from place to place to find food and land.

Persecution Ill-treating someone, often because of their religious or political beliefs.

Poncho A triangular or circular cloak with a hole in the middle for the head.

Symbol A special sign.

Tanned Soaked in a vegetable or mineral solution.

Textiles Fabric or cloth, especially when it has been woven.

Turban A head covering formed by a long, winding piece of material.

Books to read

Clothes and Costume, Nigel Nelson
  (Wayland, 1993)
Countries of the World (series)
  (Wayland)
Fibres, Science in Our World (series)
  (Earthscape Editions, 1991)
Original Peoples (series) (Wayland)
Textiles, Susie O'Reilly (Wayland, 1991)
Threatened Cultures (series) (Wayland)
Traditional Costume, Miriam Moss
  (Wayland, 1988)

Index

The costumes in this book come from many different peoples. Various types of costume are listed in the index, for example 'hats', 'dresses' and 'scarves'. If you want to see how costumes are used, look at entries such as 'ceremonies', 'dance', and 'festivals'. You can use the 'peoples' entry to look up costumes from the cultures mentioned in the book. If you are making a costume and you need some ideas, look at the 'decoration', 'design', 'materials' and 'motifs' sections.